HowExpert Presents

How To Draw People

Your Step By Step Guide To Drawing People

HowExpert with Elise White

For more tips related to this topic, visit HowExpert.com/drawpeople.

Recommended Resources

- HowExpert.com – Quick 'How To' Guides on All Topics from A to Z by Everyday Experts.
- HowExpert.com/free – Free HowExpert Email Newsletter.
- HowExpert.com/books – HowExpert Books
- HowExpert.com/courses – HowExpert Courses
- HowExpert.com/clothing – HowExpert Clothing
- HowExpert.com/membership – HowExpert Membership Site
- HowExpert.com/affiliates – HowExpert Affiliate Program
- HowExpert.com/writers – Write About Your #1 Passion/Knowledge/Expertise & Become a HowExpert Author.
- HowExpert.com/resources – Additional HowExpert Recommended Resources
- YouTube.com/HowExpert – Subscribe to HowExpert YouTube.
- Instagram.com/HowExpert – Follow HowExpert on Instagram.
- Facebook.com/HowExpert – Follow HowExpert on Facebook.

Publisher's Foreword

Dear HowExpert Reader,

HowExpert publishes quick 'how to' guides on all topics from A to Z by everyday experts.

At HowExpert, our mission is to discover, empower, and maximize talents of everyday people to ultimately make a positive impact in the world for all topics from A to Z...one everyday expert at a time!

All of our HowExpert guides are written by everyday people just like you and me who have a passion, knowledge, and expertise for a specific topic.

We take great pride in selecting everyday experts who have a passion, great writing skills, and knowledge about a topic that they love to be able to teach you about the topic you are also passionate about and eager to learn about.

We hope you get a lot of value from our HowExpert guides and it can make a positive impact in your life in some kind of way. All of our readers including you altogether help us continue living our mission of making a positive impact in the world for all spheres of influences from A to Z.

If you enjoyed one of our HowExpert guides, then please take a moment to send us your feedback from wherever you got this book.

Thank you and we wish you all the best in all aspects of life.

Sincerely,

BJ Min
Founder & Publisher of HowExpert
HowExpert.com

PS...If you are also interested in becoming a HowExpert author, then please visit our website at HowExpert.com/writers. Thank you & again, all the best!

Table of Contents

Introduction

In this guide, I will use my own pencil drawings to teach you how to draw realistic people. Like many artists, I learned to draw people by hours of practice and observation, as well as through instruction I received in my art classes in school. Personally, I do not believe that you have to have an art degree in order to be good at drawing people.

I will share with you the tips and techniques that have been beneficial to me, as I've been honing my drawing skills.

Chapter 1: Before You Begin Drawing

Recommended Drawing Materials

You will need some basic tools to get started drawing people in pencil. Here you can find my best recommendations for drawing pencils, erasers, paper and other materials.

Please consider my advice carefully, but do not feel pressured to buy everything at once. Get what you can and slowly grow your inventory of materials as you gain skill.

Lesson 1 – Best Drawing Pencils

While you are in the beginning stages of drawing people, you don't have to worry about having the array of pencils that the pros use.

In fact, in the beginning you can even just start with a regular pencil you have at home. If you're interested in making an investment into good drawing materials, go to your local craft store and purchase an inexpensive set of pencils to start, including 4B, 2B, B, 2H, and 4H pencils.

A 4B pencil has soft lead, 2B and B pencils are medium soft, 2H is medium hard, and 4H is hard lead.

As you become more comfortable and gain skill drawing with these pencils you can consider buying the full range of pencils to create more textures and effects in your drawings. Pencils come in the range of 9B - Extremely soft to 9H - Extremely hard.

Here you can see the pencil range I will be using for this guide. For simplicity, I am using 4 types of pencils that I purchased in an inexpensive set sold at my local craft store.

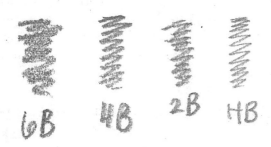

Best drawing pencils review

In Lesson 1 you learned that:

- You should start small. You don't need all the pencils the pros use when you're just beginning.
- You can start learning using any regular pencil you have around the house.
- Drawing pencils range in softness to hardness from 9B to 9H.

- Artists who use the full range of pencils use them to create effects and textures in their drawings.
- If you are interested in getting an inexpensive set of drawing pencils, you can find a good set at most craft stores.

Lesson 2 – Best Erasers

Personally, I prefer using the kneaded eraser for my drawings. As the name suggests, you can shape these erasers into the desired shape and they're great for gently lightening an area or completely removing a dark area if need be.

Kneaded erasers are easy to mold into the shape you need.

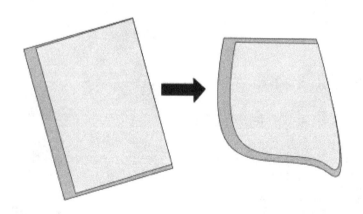

Another option that many artists like is the eraser stick. The stick is a long, pencil-like cylinder with a point that can be sliced into the needed shape, as they are quite stiff. You can also use the pointed tip like you would a pencil to draw into the graphite on the paper to create highlights and textures.

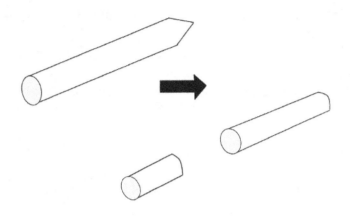

Eraser sticks are stiff and can be used like a pencil. They can be chopped to the size you want.

I do not recommend using a regular pencil's eraser for erasing or lightening your drawings. Pencil erasers were not designed for drawings, but for writing, and may smear or darken your drawing in a way you did not intend.

To avoid eraser smears on your drawings, use an eraser designed for pencil drawings.

Best erasers review

In Lesson 2 you learned that:

- You should avoid using regular erasers on your drawings, because they may leave smear marks.
- Kneaded erasers are moldable erasers that are very versatile.
- Eraser sticks can be used like pencils (with the opposite effect).
- You can also chop eraser sticks into the sizes you want.
- It is good to experiment and see which eraser you like best.

Lesson 3 – Best Drawing Paper

You can use a variety of types of paper for your pencil drawings. While you are still learning, you may want to buy a sketchbook or even just use your printer paper as you practice.

Sketchbooks provide good drawing paper to practice on.

For better quality, though, you will want to visit your local craft store and invest in higher quality paper. The surface texture of the paper affects the amount of detail and value you achieve in your drawings. You may have to experiment a bit and do your own research to find out what kind of paper best suits the type of drawing you want to create.

Hot Press Watercolor Paper, Pastel Paper, and different brands of drawing paper are good types of paper to try for finished drawings. Personally, I have used cardstock paper for some of my illustrations and have been pleased with the results. It really is a matter of preference.

Best drawing paper review

In Lesson 3 you learned that:

- In the beginning, you can use a sketchbook or printer paper to practice drawing.

- The surface texture of paper affects the way the pencil's graphite appears on the paper.
- Look at the selection available at your local craft store.
- Hot Press Watercolor Paper and Pastel Paper are favorite paper types of many artists.
- You will have to experiment and do research to find which paper works best for you.

Lesson 4 – Fixative

I highly recommend that you purchase a fixative for your finished pencil drawings. You can find it at your local craft store. It helps to prevent smearing from happening when you handle your drawings. I thought I was careful enough not to damage my drawings, and I was. I took them to be scanned so that I could make prints of them later, and the employee that made the scans got her fingerprints all over the drawings and made an indentation with the printer apparatus that left a dark mark on the paper. The whole experience really sold me on buying fixative in the future. You never know what could happen to the drawing you just worked so hard on.

One thing to bear in mind, when using spray on fixative, is safety. It is important to have good ventilation. This is another thing, I learned the hard way, when I sprayed the fixative in my bedroom with the door closed and only one window open. The smell of fixative is strong and the vapors are harmful. Go outside or into a room with circulating air and a good fan, so no one in your home or studio is subject to fumes.

Fixatives have harmful vapors, so it is better to spray your drawings outdoors or in a well-ventilated area.

Fixative review

In Lesson 4 you learned that:

- You should use fixative to avoid smudging finished drawings.
- Fixative can be purchased at your local craft store.
- Even if you are careful not to smudge your drawings, others may not be.
- The vapors from fixative are strong and harmful.
- It is important that you use fixative in a well-ventilated room or outside.

Lesson 5 – Drawing Boards and Easels

In my experience, I've noticed that it is easier for me to accurately render the proportions of a person's features, or body, when I have my drawing at an angle. Having the drawing propped up and slanting away from me helps me to have a better view of what I'm doing and, it helps me avoid distorting the person, because I'm not seeing the drawing at a good angle.

Easels aren't just for painting. They are an excellent way to prop your drawing up so that you can see what you are doing, and so that you can step back and see it as you would if it were being displayed.

Drawing boards are also very useful. I recently purchased one that had a clip at the top and a rubber band at the bottom. These help keep your drawing secure, and you can avoid touching the drawing unnecessarily with your fingers, which could cause smudges. If you prefer not to use an easel, you can use a drawing board and slant it either in your lap or workspace. Both tools are easy to take with you anywhere you'd like to spend some time drawing.

Drawing boards and easels are great for helping you see the drawing at a good angle as you work.

Drawing boards and easels review

In Lesson 5 you learned that:

- Drawing boards and easels can help you draw at a good angle.
- Using a drawing board or easel can help you avoid touching and smearing your work.
- Drawing boards have clips and bands that secure your drawing so that it doesn't move while you are drawing.
- Easels help you to visualize what the drawing will look like when it is displayed.
- You can take a drawing board or easel with you anywhere.

Lesson 6 – The Importance of Observation and Perseverance

I've found that the key to drawing people successfully is being a good observer. If you want to create a drawing that realistically depicts a person, it's important to get a sense of the person's personality. Even if you are looking at a photograph of someone you have never met, by looking at their expressions, pose and dress you can learn a lot about the subject's personality.

Perseverance

Maybe drawing doesn't come naturally to you. It may require effort and not come as easily as you want it to. Of course, this eBook is designed to help you draw people better and with less frustration. Still, it will take practice to get truly comfortable drawing people and understanding how to get the desired effects with the pencil.

As you go through the process, stay positive and know that you will get it. Don't give up. Keep trying.

Here you can see one of my early pencil drawings, and one of my more recent drawings. See any progress?

The lesson is - just relax. You don't have to be perfect from the beginning. Just keep trying.

The importance of observation and perseverance review

In Lesson 6 you learned that:

- The key to drawing people successfully is being a good observer.
- When you are creating a drawing, try to get a sense of your subject's personality.
- Although this eBook is designed to make drawing easier for you, it will still require effort on your part.
- It takes practice for you to be able to feel comfortable drawing people.
- When it gets challenging, stay positive and don't give up.

Chapter 2: Drawing the Parts of The Face

In this section you will learn to draw the different parts of the face, such as the eyes, nose and mouth. Learning how to draw the face is a good starting point, as you work toward being able to draw people realistically.

You will also learn how these different parts can be rendered proportionally on the face.

Lesson 1 – Drawing Eyes

We will start with the basic steps to drawing the eyes.

First, I will show you how to draw one eye and focus on the parts of the eye that your drawing should portray.

I like to start my drawings with the eyes. The eyes are located in the middle of the face, as shown in the simple diagram below.

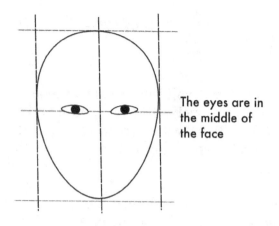

The eyes are in the middle of the face

Let's zero in on the important details of the structure of the eye. Here I've created a helpful simple diagram of the parts of the eye:

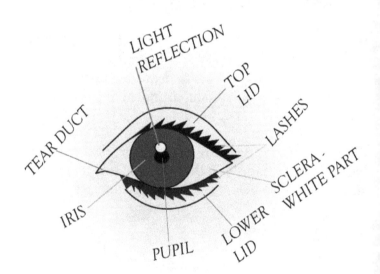

Remembering these main parts of the eye will help you to draw realistic eyes.

Other parts of note are the eye socket, cornea, glabella, brow ridge, and epicanthic fold.

Here's a short and sweet explanation of each of them.

The eye socket refers to the curved depression in the skeleton where the eyeball sits.

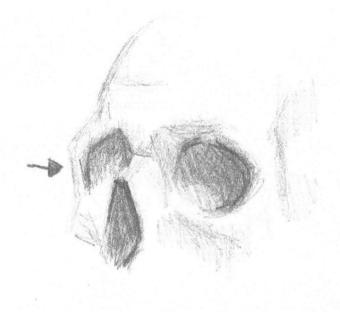

The cornea is a convex form that is over the iris. The cornea affects the shape of the lid as the eye moves, since it pushes against the skin of the lid.

The glabella is the smooth part of the forehead between the eyebrows. It is also referred to as the third eye. Here you can see mine.

The epicanthic fold is a fold of skin from the upper eyelid that can cover the inner angle of the eye. You may notice this when drawing someone of Asian descent.

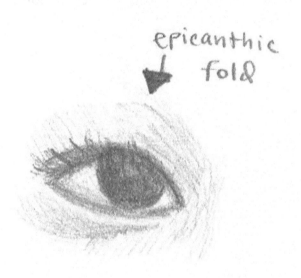

The eye in profile

When you view someone's eye in profile, really all you see is the skin around the eye, and the curve of the eye itself.

To draw an eye in profile, make the lids and lashes by creating an open triangle. The top lid is longer than the bottom lid, since it hangs over more to protect the eye.

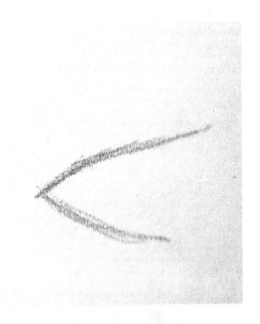

Draw a curved line for the visible part of the eyeball.

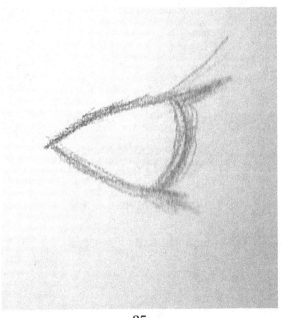

Draw a vertical line behind the curved line. Fill in the end to create the colored part of the eye, the iris. Save your drawing of the eye in profile, because we will be adding a brow ridge and brows later.

Drawing the eye straight on

Below, we will practice drawing one eye straight on.

The top lid has three planes.

And the bottom lid has two planes.

Next, I start to work in the outline of the iris and add more definition to the lids. Be very observant of either your photo or live reference. The position of the iris in their eye affects where they will be gazing in your picture to a degree.

I make sure to look closely at my reference, and then I begin to add shading to the iris. I also add shading to the sclera. Even though it is called the "white of the eye," it should not be drawn completely white. Remember, the eye is a ball and you need to draw it with some shading to show that it is spherical and three-dimensional.

You don't see many lashes in my drawing and that's
because my reference is looking down slightly and the
shadow darkens the area around her eyes.

I color in the iris, or colored part of the eye, darkly. Usually I leave a white circle where the light reflects off of the eye. There usually is a highlight visible on the eye, because of the transparent cornea that is over the iris. The highlight will always be on the dark side of the iris.

Adding the brow ridge, brows, and glabella

Let's go back to the eye you drew in profile. You will want to add a brow ridge to the drawing. The brow ridge sticks out above the eye like an awning does over a window. So make sure that you don't make the ridge flat.

To create the brow ridge, I draw a line slanting up from the top of the upper eyelid, which then curves up. We have a brow ridge, because of the brow bone underneath and because of the way the skeleton is shaped around the eye socket.

I also drew a line beneath the lower eyelid to add more to its shape.

I also made a line curving down and away from the brow ridge to create the top of the nose or glabella.

To add the eyebrow, I draw a line from the brow ridge slanting slightly upward over the eye area. This line is highlighted in red to make it easy to identify for teaching purposes.

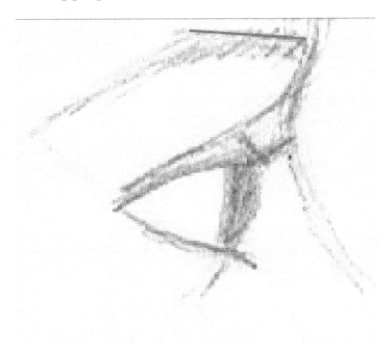

Next, I add a slanting line that lines up with the triangular shape the lid makes with the brow ridge.

The line is shown in blue. A dashed line shows how the end of the brow and the peak of the lid meet up.

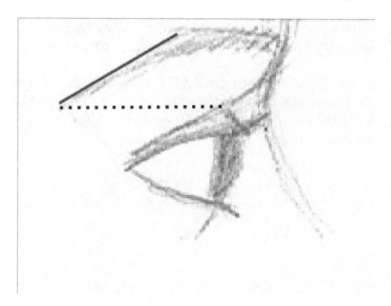

Then I draw an arcing line from the tip of the last line I drew; this is shown by the green line in the image.

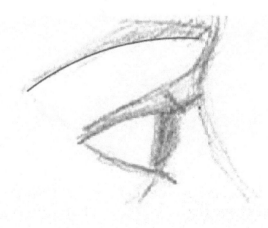

Then I connect the arcing line to the first line I drew with a small line slanting forward. This line is shown in orange in the image.

After that, I shade the eyebrow, imitating the way the hairs lay, with lines similar to the one shown before in orange.

People have many different types of brows, so do not expect to always draw them to look this way. Some people have very dark, thick brows. The brows may seem to connect with hair going between the brows across the glabella. On the other hand, other people have very little to no eyebrow hair. You have to be alert to these differences when drawing.

Before we start adding the brow area to the eye you drew in the straight on view, let's add another eye.

Take the eye that you've drawn and use that eye as your standard measurement. Add another eye, about an eye's width apart from your first eye. Sort of like this; except you'll do yours with an imaginary third eye in between for your measurement:

Here's my second eye. I used the same process that I used with the first eye.

Now let's start adding the brows.

The brow sits on the brow ridge. It will peak toward the outside end, and the outer end of the brow will often be lighter and have less hair. So I started with the bottom of the eyebrow. There are 2 lines; the first starts near the eye and peaks up, and the second is almost straight across.

Next, I add the top portion of the brow. There are three lines I draw for the top of the brow.

When drawing men, you will probably notice that their eyebrows are often fuller and straighter, while women's brows are thinner and may have a higher peak. I am drawing a woman's eyes and brows.

As I fill in the brows, I try to observe the direction the hairs lay. My subject's brows are thick and the hairs are long. Her hairs actually go down towards her eyes. I found that interesting, since my own brow hairs go up away from my eyes.

Drawing different types of eyes

There are many different types of eyes. Here are some quick sketches of examples of the various types below (Notice how I use shading to show the positioning of the eye in relation to the nose and brows):

Standard Eyes – The distance between each eye is equal to the width of one eye. The lids are visible and have the same dimension from one side to the other.

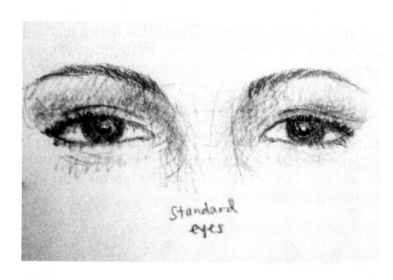

Standard eyes

Wide-set Eyes – Eyes that are more than the width of one eye apart.

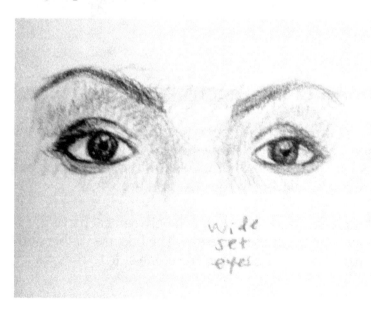

wide set eyes

Close-set Eyes – Eyes that are less than the width of one eye apart.

close set eyes

Deep-set Eyes – Eyes that are set beneath the brow.

deepset eyes

Prominent Eyes – Eyes that protrude and have heavy lids

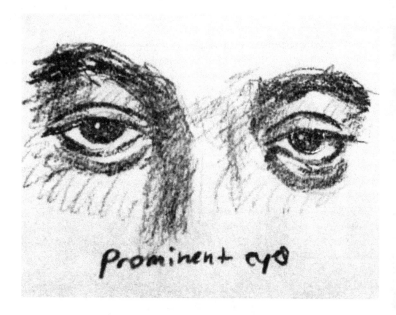

Hooded Eyes – We see that the epicanthic fold is covering the inner corner of the top lid like a hood.

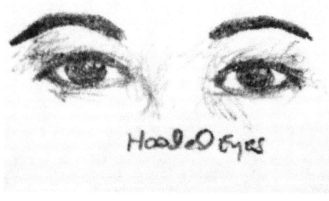

Droopy Eyes– Eyes that seem to droop down at the sides.

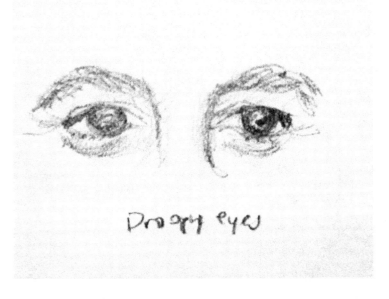

Drawing eyes review

In Lesson 1 you learned that:

- The eyes are positioned in the middle of the head.
- Shading is important for drawing the eyes, to create the lids and the round shape of the eye.
- The eye in profile looks like a triangle with a rounded base.
- There are different types of eyes.
- Most eyes are about an eye's width apart.

Lesson 2 – Drawing Ears

The ears line up with the placement of the eyes in the middle of the head. The top of the ears lines up with the brow line and the bottom lines up with the base of the nose. You can see how the ears and eyes fit together proportionally in this diagram.

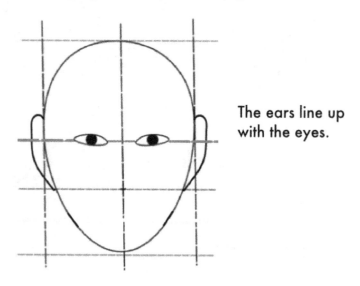

The ears line up with the eyes.

Let's draw the ear from profile view. In this view, more of the parts of the ear are visible. For that reason, drawing the ear can be intimidating. There are a lot of shapes that maybe seem strange and difficult to replicate. I saw a great suggestion on a way to break it down.

The curvature of the outline of the ear resembles a question mark, doesn't it? The inner part of the ear looks like a "y" shape. So think of those two shapes when it all seems too confusing.

If you want to know a little more about what to call those strange shapes in the ear, this diagram should help. I drew it from my own ear.

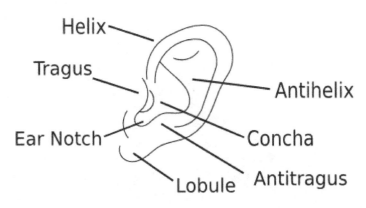

First, we'll start with a simple, open egg shape, similar to the shape of the head. Draw it at a slight slant, like my image.

Next, I make a line inside of the oval that is similar to the outer outline. This is the helix as represented by the red line in the image below.

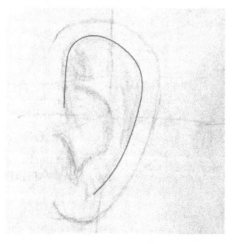

Then I draw in the curved line in the inner middle of the ear. The blue line shows this curve, which is part of the antihelix.

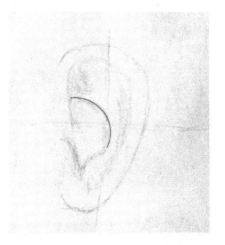

Then I draw in three more arcs for the depression in the upper part of the antihelix, and for the tragus and antitragus. You can see these arcs in orange.

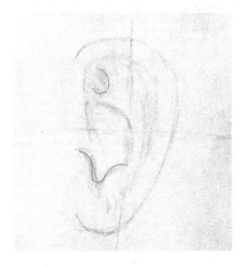

After I have the main shapes of the ear drawn in, I focus on shading.

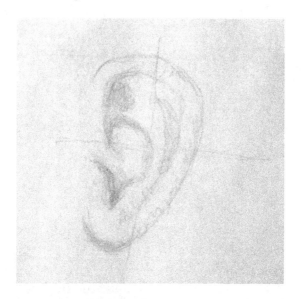

I make the depression in the antihelix darker and add some shading to the side of the antihelix along the helix. I also shade the tragus, antitragus, and the bottom of the lobule.

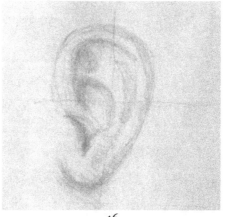

Then, I give more attention to shading the outer part of the helix, to make the ear appear more three-dimensional. I also add some shadow to the concha and below the lobule.

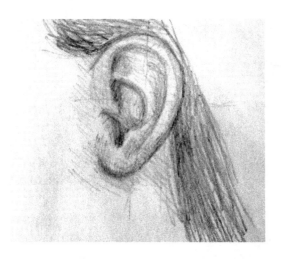

Here you can see that I continued shading, observing my subject to see what areas had the darkest shadows. I've added hair here, but you don't have to worry about adding it in. We'll work on drawing hair in another chapter.

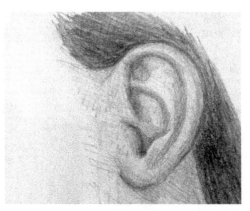

In this last image, I've finished the ear by smoothing and blending my shading a bit more. I use the cross-hatching shading method. I make my lines intersect over and over, doing it more in darker shaded areas. Sometimes, I'll take my finger or a tissue, if I want the drawing to be smooth.

Drawing ears review

In Lesson 2 you learned that:

- The ears are positioned between the brow line and the base of the nose.
- In profile, the ear looks like a question mark with a "y" inside.
- The ear slants backward.
- The overall shape of the ear is like an egg.
- You can smooth your shading with a tissue.

Lesson 3 – Drawing Noses

The nose is located in the middle of the lower half of the face, between the eyes.

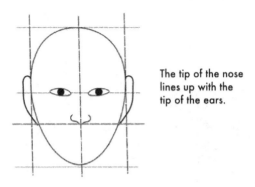

The tip of the nose lines up with the tip of the ears.

When we break down the nose into its basic shape, it's like an open oval and three circles. The open oval is the length of the nose, the largest circle is the tip and the smaller two circles are the nostrils. Lightly draw the four shapes on your paper. Don't worry about making perfect circles, since we will only be using circles as the base for our drawing.

Here are my open oval and circles.

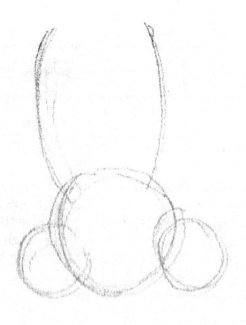

Next, I start shading in the shadows, I see on the sides of the oval part of the nose. If you can grab a photo to use, I recommend grabbing that so you can add realistic shadow to your nose.

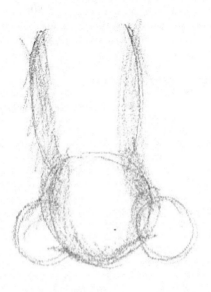

Notice that I did not just make a dark outline to show the sides of the nose. If you are looking at a photo reference or live model, you will see that shadow is what creates the visual boundaries of the nose.

Next, I continue to shade the nose, especially in the darkest part, the nostrils.

It's starting to look more like a nose now, isn't it? I started to make defining lines on the nostrils, tip of the nose, and sides of the nostrils. There is more of a visible outline here than there is on the side of the length or bridge of the nose.

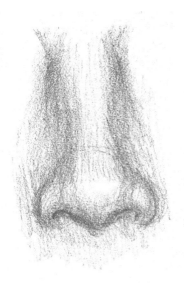

When finishing the nose, I paid attention to adding more shading and leaving white spots for the highlights on the nose.

Depending on the look that you want, and the rest of your drawing, you can continue shading the nose to create dramatic contrast. Since this nose is for demonstration purposes only, I'll wrap up my nose drawing here.

All noses are not the same, so the placement of your open oval and circles really depends on your subject. With some people, it is easy to see the inside of their nostrils, when they are facing you straight on; while with others who may have longer noses, you may not see the inside of the nostrils when they're facing you.

Now let's work on drawing a nose in profile.

Drawing noses review

In Lesson 3 you learned that:

- From straight on, the nose consists of an open oval, and three circles.
- Shading is important, for drawing the eyes, to create the lids and the round shape of the eye.
- The eye in profile looks like a triangle with a rounded base.
- There are different types of eyes.
- Most eyes are about an eye's width apart.

Lesson 4 – Drawing Mouths

The mouth is positioned in the middle of the space below the nose.

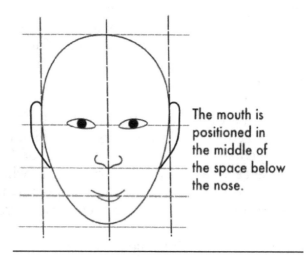

The mouth is positioned in the middle of the space below the nose.

The lips can be broken down into four basic shapes, an equilateral triangle and three circles.

You may wonder where I'm going with this, but just follow along.

Add a center line between the top circle and the circles below. This is the center line of the mouth.

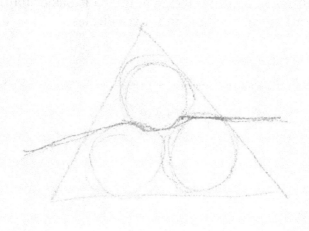

Next, add a line that slants up to the top circle, and dips down into it and down the other side of the circle. This is the top lip, and the dip is the depression above your lip called the Cupid's bow.

Now add the bottom lip, going beneath and slanting up the sides of the two bottom circles.

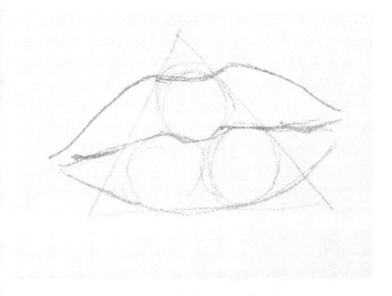

Now you should have a pair of recognizable lips. From here we can add in more detail. I shade the top and bottom lips, starting from where they meet in the center. I try to convey the rounded shape of the lips.

I also add shading to the top of the top lip and the bottom of the bottom lip. There is a highlight in the middle of each lip, so I let more of the white paper show through.

I continue to shade the lips, to show that the lips curve.

I'm drawing Angelina Jolie's lips, which look puckered up a lot of the time. The size and roundness of the lips varies from person to person. Some people seem to barely have lips. So you will have to note the shape of their lips and the size when drawing.

Here, I've finished shading the lips and the Cupid's bow. When drawing lips, be observant of the creases that the lips have and lightly work them in.

Drawing teeth

Drawing teeth can be tricky, and even intimidating. I remember that at one time, I would try to avoid it all together, for fear of messing up the rest of the portrait with some bad teeth.

I think part of what makes drawing teeth difficult is the perception that we have in our minds. When I watched cartoons and saw people's teeth either shown as a white strip, or a series of rectangles, it created an unrealistic idea of how to portray teeth in my mind.

A good artist is a good observer. Instead of relying on what your mind says teeth should look like, you have to look at the actual teeth and draw what you see.

Here I am beginning to draw some teeth. The basic sketch is there of the lips and teeth.

The man I was drawing did not have perfect teeth. In fact, he had some gold teeth. Here you can see that I tried not to shade the teeth too darkly, yet I tried not to make them appear flat and white. You have to find a good balance in your drawings and really observe the teeth of your subject.

Drawing mouths review

In Lesson 4 you learned that:

- The basic shapes that can guide you in drawing the mouth are three circles and a triangle.
- The depression above the top lip is called the Cupid's bow.
- Lips are rounded, so shading should convey that.
- The mouth is located in the middle of the space beneath the nose.
- You can smooth your shading with a tissue.

Chapter 3: Drawing Faces

In this chapter, we put it all together. You will work on gaining further understanding on how the eyes, nose, ears, and mouth fit proportionally on the face.

You will also learn how to draw a face from different perspectives.

Lesson 1 – Drawing a Face Straight On

Here is a basic diagram I've made of how the parts of the face should fit together proportionally from a straight on view.

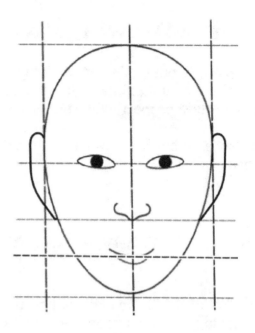

The basic shapes of the head

The head is a sphere and a block. Here they are from the side.

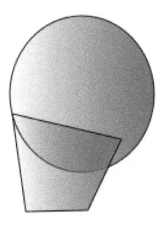

The sphere has its sides cut off, because the head is flat on the sides. It's a good idea to practice drawing these two shapes, since they represent the structure of the head. Once you understand the basic structure, it will be easier for you to draw the features accurately on the head, and from different angles.

Be observant of how many "eye widths" distance there are, in different features of your subject - using the measurement of their eye - if it doesn't match up with your drawing, you need to make an adjustment. This measurement is preferably done in the beginning, that way you can save yourself some grief later when you discover things don't quite match up.

Here is a man that I drew in the straight on view. I think drawing people straight on is probably the easiest way, when you are beginning to draw. It is easy to figure out how the facial features should relate to one another. I made sure that his ears lined up with his brows and the base of his nose. I also checked his other proportions, like the placement of his eyes and mouth. Even though people may look different from one another, we are made the same way and you will be able to see that our faces all follow the same general rules.

Why don't you try referencing this drawing and the diagram at the beginning of this lesson, along with a reference photo of your choice, and try drawing some people straight on?

Drawing a face straight on review

In Lesson 1 you learned that:

- The basic shapes of the head are a sphere and a block.
- The eye width is a good standard measurement for the face.
- It is better to measure beforehand, than it is to do it after you've worked on your drawing for a while.
- The proportions of the face apply to everyone, despite our different characteristics.
- Drawing people straight on is easy!

Lesson 2 – Drawing Faces from Different Perspectives

Now that you feel more comfortable drawing the face, we will work on drawing the face from different perspectives or angles.

The three most common perspectives that portraits are drawn in are:

Straight on, Profile and Three Quarters

Straight on

Profile

69

Three Quarters

We've already worked on drawing a face from the straight on view. So we will primarily discuss drawing a face in profile and three quarter view. Practice each exercise, until you feel comfortable with how your drawings are turning out.

Drawing a Face in Profile View

We covered drawing the eye and brow area in profile, in an earlier lesson. So you've had a bit of practice with drawing the face in profile.

To get started, remember your proportions. These proportions are great to fall back on, when you are drawing the head from different views. The head can be divided into three equal sections:

- The hairline to the brow
- The brow to the bottom of the nose
- The bottom of the nose to the chin

For drawing in profile, a few other measurements and tips will be helpful to you. Practice putting these measurements to work:

- The corner of the lip lines up with the front of the eye.
- The bottom lip (where it meets the chin) lines up with the jawline.
- The neck is slanted forward, not straight up and down.
- The ear slants backward, along with the part of the jaw that slants up.

I'll start with an outline of the general shape of the head. Remember the head is a sphere and a block.

I keep in mind the guidelines I just mentioned and make sure that the head is equally divisible by three. I've included light lines, for you to see this measurement. As you practice, you may want to include these lines as well; drawing them lightly, so that you can go back and erase later or shade over it.

I add the brow and eye first, then I add the nose and ear.

I make sure to line the slant of the ear up with the slant of the upper part of the jaw.

Next, I add in the lips, chin and tweak the jaw line. I make sure that the corner of the mouth lines up with the front of the eye.

I also check that the bottom of the lip lines up with the point where the jaw begins to go up vertically.

Then I tweak the sketch of the neck and add any details I want.

Drawing a Face in Three-Quarter View

Out of the three most common perspectives – three quarter is probably the most intimidating. That's because we've got a bit of foreshortening going on.

Foreshortening, if you're wondering, means to shorten the parts of an object (such as the side of the face, that is turned at an angle away from you), to create the illusion of three-dimensional space.

Despite the perceived difficulty, three quarter view is one of the most common ways that we see the face drawn. So that should be encouraging that it's more than doable. Plus, you're armed with your understanding of the basic structure of the face and its proportions.

You will see a few differences:

- The distance between the eyes may be less than one eye, instead of one, as you're used to seeing.

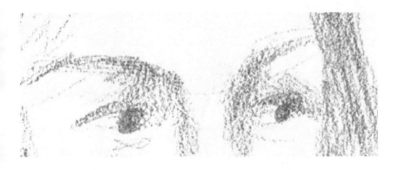

- The eyes may be opened to different degrees.
- The sides of the mouth will appear differently from one another.

- Only one ear may be visible.
- Due to the angle, the sides of the face will also appear differently.

Although the eyes seem closer from this view, you can still use the eye (the full eye on the near side), as your standard measurement. It is even more important to measure, in three quarter view, than it was in straight on and profile.

Here is a girl that I drew who is a good example of a face in three quarter view.

Drawing faces from different perspectives review

In Lesson 2 you learned that:

- The three most common perspectives are straight on, profile, and three quarters.
- Three quarter view involves foreshortening.
- Foreshortening means to shorten parts of the object for the illusion of three-dimensional space.
- Three quarter view is probably the most common view for portraits.
- It is very important to use standard measurements in profile and three quarter view.

Chapter 4: Drawing Hair and Facial Hair

Now that you know how to draw faces, you can work on mastering drawing different hairstyles. Just as there are many different types of eyes, noses and ears; there are many, if not more, types of hairstyles. So in this chapter, we will work on drawing more than one type of hairstyle; so that you can get a feel for drawing the variety that is out there.

Before we get started, bear this important point in mind. You may have realized this already (or you may have noticed that I mentioned this before), but the key to drawing realistically is to draw what you really see. So as we practice drawing hair, focus on drawing the values and shapes that are seen. Look for what is dark and what is light, in the photo that you are drawing from, or as you observe your model.

I start with the dark values first and then work in the lighter areas. For each different hair type, you will notice that both the values and the lines are important, to show the flow of the hair. Don't worry about trying to draw every strand of hair. Do draw a few individual hairs, where it seems appropriate.

Lesson 1 – Drawing Straight Hair

We will start with drawing a woman who has straight hair. I start with sketching out how the hair lays around the face.

Then I work on shading the hair more, especially in the darker spots, and I leave white areas of the paper where the highlights of the hair are.

The subject for this drawing had a choppy haircut, so I made choppy lines. You can be expressive and have fun when drawing hair. It adds a lot to your drawing. Even though you are working on drawing people realistically feel free to put your own spin on things.

Drawing straight hair review

In Lesson 1 you learned that:

- Start your drawing by noticing how the hair lays around the face.
- Look for where the highlights are in the hair.
- Do less shading and let the paper show through, in places where there are highlights.
- Draw with lines that imitate the way the hair lays.
- You can put your own spin on your drawings, even though you want to make them a likeness of your subject.

Lesson 2 – Drawing Wavy Hair

Here I am drawing a woman with long wavy hair. So I will make more flowing marks instead of the choppy ones I used in the last lesson.

First, I lightly sketch out the direction the hair is going. It is important to see what the flow of the hair is, especially with longer hair.

flow of hair

We can see that since she is leaning, her hair is flowing in the direction that she is leaning.

Here I've added more shading. I observed where the hair was darkest and where the highlights were. You don't have to draw every strand of hair. Just try to make it appear like hair and convey whatever you want to with it.

I also noticed that her hair was slightly layered and it wasn't all the same length, so I made some lines shorter than others.

Drawing wavy hair review

In Lesson 2 you learned that:

- Use curvy lines for wavy hair.
- If your subject is leaning, notice how that affects the flow of the hair.
- You do not have to draw every strand of hair.
- Look for where the hair is the darkest.
- Notice whether, or not the hair is the same length.

Lesson 3 – Drawing Curly Hair

Curly hair is similar to wavy hair, except the curls are tighter. Here I've drawn a sketch of my own hair.

Drawing hair takes planning. I enjoy drawing intricate styles. If that's not your cup of tea, maybe you should go for hair that has less texture, like straight or wavy hair.

For more examples of curly hair, check out Chapter 6, Lesson 6 about drawing different ethnicities.

Drawing curly hair review

In Lesson 3 you learned that:

- Curly hair is similar to wavy hair but has tighter curls.
- Decide whether, or not you like to draw intricate hair styles.
- Have a plan for how you will draw the hair.
- The more textured the hair is, the more time it takes to draw.
- If you don't like spending time on drawing the hair, plan to draw hair that is not highly textured.

Lesson 4 – Drawing Male Pattern Baldness

Even bald men can have a lot of different hairstyles. There's the infamous comb-over, for instance. I've even seen men who have ponytails and they have no hair in the front.

Here I've drawn a balding man and the hair that he does have is very short. Make sure you draw enough of the forehead for a balding man, since his hairline is receded.

I kept the lines very short. I noticed that the man that I was drawing had a spot, on the top left side of his head, which was reflecting the light source. So I left that portion of his head white. That would be more visible, if I made this a finished drawing. When you draw someone who is bald or balding, be aware that there may be highlights on their heads.

Drawing male pattern baldness review

In Lesson 4 you learned that:

- There are actually different styles that balding men can wear.
- You should watch out for highlights on the top of balding men's heads.
- Make sure you draw enough of the forehead for a balding man.

Lesson 5 – Drawing Facial Hair

Drawing facial hair is a lot like drawing hair. Men have it in varying degrees. Some just have a bit of stubble, while others may have a beard that makes them look a bit like Santa Claus.

In this lesson, I will show you how I draw a man with a short mustache and beard.

Here he starts out clean-shaven, with just a bit of shadow by his jaw line.

Then I work in a bit of a mustache and goatee. I do this with short straight lines that form the desired shapes.

I continue to draw the short lines in the shape of his beard. I make the beard darker under his chin. The subject for this drawing had hair on his neck as well.

So be aware that you may be drawing hair on their neck and not just their face.

Drawing facial hair review

In Lesson 5 you learned that:

- Facial hair can come in a variety of lengths.
- If the hair is short, use very short lines.
- Work the lines into the shape you want for the mustache or beard.
- Notice if the hair is visible on the neck.
- Notice if the hair is darker in different spots.

Chapter 5: Drawing the Body

Drawing the human body requires the use of your powers of observation and an understanding of anatomy. You don't have to know what each bone and tendon is called in the body, and you don't have to make a thousand drawings of skeletons, to learn to draw the body successfully. But you do need to understand how the parts of the body should be drawn in proportion to one another.

One of the greatest things about choosing people as your subjects is that they're everywhere. So try this beginning exercise. Look at a photo or ask someone around you to stand and pose for a moment. Take mental notes of how long their arms reach, in comparison to the rest of their body from the shoulders down. Notice the length of their legs and torso. Look at the width of the shoulders on either side of their neck.

Try to map out what you observed, by drawing a quick sketch on paper. It may not be perfect, but taking mental notes about how the person's body parts fit together is sure to stick in your mind and help you draw that much better the next time you draw someone's body.

Breaking down the body parts into basic shapes

If you plan to create a drawing of someone from head to toe, it is a good idea to sketch out their form. That way you won't run out of space and have to start all over or revise your original plan.

An adult is approximately 8 heads high, so when we are drawing the body, the length of the head will be our standard measurement, like the eye was for the face.

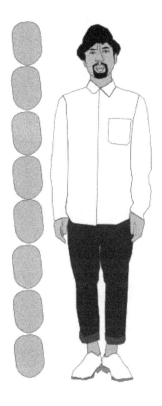

If you can, pull up a picture of the human skeleton. This will be a helpful reference to you, since the skeleton provides the underlying structure of the body.

The skeleton can be broken down into these basic shapes:

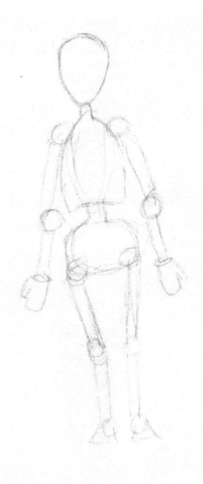

This drawing looks similar to the wooden poseable figures many artists use to help them draw their figures in different poses. It wouldn't be a bad idea to purchase one of these if you can. They are great to use for practicing drawing the human form.

Here is the body from the side. So that you can see the curvature of the spine, the arms are not added.

How to Draw Hands

Here is my rough sketch of the hand. Some things to keep in mind are that, like the face, the hand can be divided into equal parts.

Here I've divided the hand from the wrist to the knuckles and from the knuckles to the tips of the fingers.

It's up to you, how big a part of your drawing you want the hand to be. Some people like to add a lot of detail to hands. If you choose to do that, be mindful of the shadows on the hand.

Here, I've drawn a hand in a relaxed position. When the fingers are bent, the fingers may be foreshortened, so you may have to draw the fingers, and different angles, where they look shorter than the fingers that are not foreshortened.

Drawing the body review

In Chapter 5 you learned that:

- Most adults are 8 heads tall.
- The head is a good standard measurement for the body.
- The hand can be divided in two equal parts.
- Hands can be your focal point or just a small part of your drawing.
- You may use foreshortening in drawing bent fingers.

Chapter 6: Drawing Different Types of People

In the last chapter, we covered the fundamentals of drawing the form of the human body. Now we will practice drawing different types of people and learn to identify strategies for portraying them accurately.

Lesson 1 – Drawing Adults

We hear a lot about women's curves and that's because the basic shapes in a woman's body are circles and ovals.

Men tend to be more angular than women. So think of squares and rectangles.

Here I've drawn an example of a man from the back and the front.

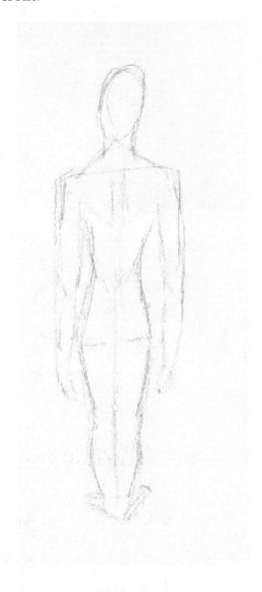

Lesson 2 – Drawing Children

Drawing children is similar to drawing adults. A child, of course, is shorter, and they will be less than 8 heads in proportion to their body. Their heads are bigger in proportion to their bodies than adults' heads are.

Here is an example of a child that I drew.

When you are drawing children, think about the differences in how they look, especially in the face, in comparison to adults and draw accordingly. You don't want what was supposed to be a child to look more like a little man or woman. Children have wide eyes and rounder faces than adults.

Drawing children review

In Lesson 2 you learned that:

- Children are not 8 heads tall.
- Children have bigger heads in proportion to their bodies than adults do.
- Children have round features.
- You should work on noticing the differences between how kids and adults look.
- If you draw children the way you draw adults, they'll look like a dwarf instead of a child.

Lesson 3 – Drawing Babies

When drawing a baby, you can use circles and ovals. Babies usually don't have much of a visible neck, so you can simply start with a circle for the head that attaches to a bigger oval, the torso of the baby.

I also added in the arms and feet. If you draw a baby, it isn't very likely you'll draw it standing. This baby is sitting with his legs folded in front of him and his arms at his side.

Here, I've added the facial features of the baby.
Babies' eyes appear to be larger in comparison with
their mouths and noses than adult's eyes do. Their
faces and really their whole bodies are rounder and
chubbier than most adults' bodies.

Drawing babies review

In Lesson 3 you learned that:

- Babies are circles and ovals.
- You aren't likely to draw a standing baby.
- Babies have big eyes in proportion to the rest of their bodies.
- Look for where the hair is the darkest.
- Babies don't really have a visible neck.
- Babies have chubby faces.

Lesson 4 – Drawing the Elderly

Really, everyone has wrinkles to some degree. Think about it; laugh lines and smile lines, they're just folds that our skin makes when we move our facial muscles a certain way.

Of course, the elderly have a lot more wrinkles than younger people do. This can be a challenge to draw, since their skin may have a rougher, wrinkly texture on more than just their face. This requires you to be observant of the lights and darks on their skin, so you can accurately convey the texture.

Here I've drawn an elderly woman with creased skin. I start with laying out the most visible lines on her face.

Then I add shading and the finer lines. I add the fine lines lightly. Notice how this lady's skin is drooping over her eyes and even her ear looks droopy? It is important to notice the makeup of the skin.

Drawing the elderly review

In Lesson 4 you learned that:

- Everyone has wrinkles.
- Start with the wrinkle lines, which are most visible.
- Draw the fine lines lightly.
- It is important to notice the makeup of the skin.
- The elderly may have wrinkles and rough skin in places other than their faces, as well.

Lesson 5 – Drawing People of Different Ethnicities

I enjoy drawing people from a variety of places. That means that I get to draw lots of different features.

I've learned that it's good to start a drawing with an open mind. Each person is unique. I try not to generalize about how to portray different ethnicities. In this lesson, we'll look at three features in which you may notice variations.

Skin Color

Drawing people of different skin colors really isn't that much of a challenge when working with pencil. It really just requires more, or less, shading.

Here I've drawn an African American man I saw on the website, The Sartorialist. I like to use it to find interesting pictures to draw from.

This image is at the point where I was just beginning to lay down some shading.

Here he is after I've worked more shading in.

This drawing was made for this guide; but if it was one, I wanted to finish, I would continue shading to make his face smoother and to add more contrast. This does give you the general idea, though.

Facial Features

In the lesson about eyes, I mentioned the epicanthic fold. That is a feature, which you may have noticed, that many people of Asian descent have.

Here it is again.

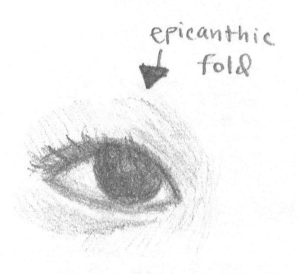

epicanthic
fold

Remember to avoid generalizing and to really study the features of your subject.

Notice the eyes of the lady with the straight hair that I drew for the lesson on straight hair.

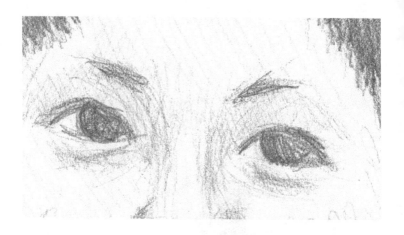

Sometimes people, who are not of Asian descent, may have eyes that you would think you would see on an Asian person. There are no set features for each ethnicity or nationality. Keep an open mind.

Hair

As we discussed, there are many types of hair, and people use many different hairstyles to try and change it.

Like facial features, each ethnic group does not have default hair.

I will show you some examples of hair for African American people that I have drawn.

Here, you see a portion of hair, from a drawing I did of an African American woman, who styled her hair in two, thick-strand twists, and then untwisted it, to create these chunky curls.

This next image shows a portion of hair from a drawing I did of the singer Corinne Bailey Rae. She braids her hair into plaits at night and then unbraids it for her flowing curls.

Then we have the drawing I did of the African American man and his short-cut hair.

Do you see the variety that exists just in one ethnic group? So be observant and enjoy drawing the unique people out there in the world.

Drawing people of different ethnicities review

In Lesson 5 you learned that:

- You shouldn't make generalizations about the features of different ethnicities.
- Drawing different skin colors just involves how much you shade.
- The epicanthic fold is common among people of Asian descent and even among other races.
- There are many types of curly hair.
- You will have success if you keep an open mind.

Chapter 7: Drawing Articles of Clothing

While people are in the beginning stages of learning to draw realistically, one of the biggest challenges they face is drawing clothing, without making it appear flat and unrealistic. In this chapter, you will learn how to portray the different types of clothing and accessories that your subjects may be wearing.

You may find that you enjoy drawing clothing, since it can add expressiveness to your work.

Lesson 1 – Drawing Clothing

When drawing clothing, you need to be aware of the major folds caused by the body movements beneath the clothing.

For instance, the major folds in shirts are caused by the elbow and armpits.

Before drawing the clothing, think about the form underneath.

Here I began adding the clothes over the form.

Here I've drawn a young guy in a sweat, jeans, and sneakers. I looked for where his shirt and pants were creased and folded and the shadows that the folds created.

Drawing clothing review

In Lesson 3 you learned that:

- You should look for the major folds.
- Remember the form underneath the clothing.
- Body movements cause the folds in clothes.
- Look for creases and folds when shading.

Lesson 2 – Drawing Accessories

If you are drawing women, you are bound to draw accessories sometime.

First let's look at how to draw hats.

I saw a photo of a stylish lady with a brown hat on. First, I sketched out how the hat looked and how its size compared to her head.

I noticed that the hat covered a good portion of her forehead, but it wasn't much wider than her hair.

Here you can see that I added more shading. The brim of the hat casts shadows over the top of her face. I also noticed that the brim had a highlight around the tip, where it turns up toward the light. There were also two dents, toward the top of the hat, which I made sure to shade.

Here is a woman with a purse. When drawing her, I noticed how her hand grasped the straps and the form of the bag. It's a rectangular purse, but to only draw a rectangle would make it flat. I looked for places to shade the purse to add dimension.

Drawing accessories review

In Lesson 4 you learned that:

- When drawing hats, look at how big they are in comparison to the head.
- You should notice how the hat affects the shading of the face.
- You should look for highlights on the hat.
- When drawing purses, even if they are a simple shape, be sure to add shading so they won't be flat.
- Observe how the woman holds the handles of the purse, so you can make it appear life-like.

Lesson 3 – Drawing Footwear

Drawing footwear may seem daunting at first. As you've learned throughout this guide, breaking down things into simpler shapes can be very helpful.

I remember thinking that drawing heels was challenging. I think it was because of how they appear from the front view. Let's practice drawing them.

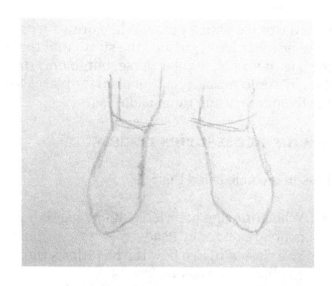

Here we can see that the basic shapes are two rectangles and a triangle.

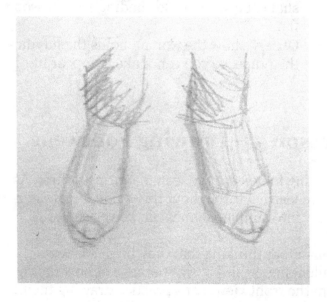

After you figure out the basic shapes of the shoes, you just have to work in the shading.

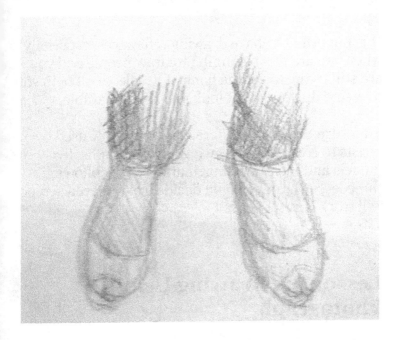

Then you have some stylish peep-toes to go with the stylish lady you've been drawing.

Chapter 8: Using Drawing References

It is important to have drawing references, especially when you are just beginning to draw people and you are still trying to get the hang of it. These will help you to create drawings that look real and believable.

There are three main references commonly used by artists to create their drawings: photographs, live models and their own imaginations. The following three lessons can help you decide what reference type will work best for you.

Lesson 1 – Drawing Using a Photograph

Drawing from a photo reference is the way many beginners start drawing people and some professional artists even prefer this method.

What are the benefits of using photos as references?

- Unlike live models, you don't have to worry about your photo moving out of the position you were drawing it in.
- You can take a photo anywhere and refer to it at any time.
- If you are using a computer to view the photo, you can zoom in on details that you'd like to see clearer.

- If you have access to a projector, you can project the photo onto a wall and draw over the projected image.

If you decide to use this method, be sure to choose a good reference photo. Make sure that it is large enough for you to see the details of the subject you want to draw. I like to use photos on my computer so that I can zoom in and toggle the photo as much as I want.

Also make sure that the photo you've chosen is interesting to you, so that you won't get bored and quit the drawing. You can find good photos to draw from in magazines, on the Internet, and even in family photo albums.

I recommend drawing from a photograph that you've uploaded to your computer, so that you can control how you view the photo as you draw.

Drawing using a photograph review

In Lesson 1 you learned that:

- Using a photo as a drawing reference is the easiest choice.
- It is important to use a photo that interests you.
- You should make sure that your photo is clear and large enough for you to see important details.
- You can find good photos in magazines, on the Internet, and in family photo albums.

- You can upload photos to your computer, so that you can zoom in and see details of the photo more clearly.

Lesson 2 – Drawing Using a Live Model

Creating a drawing by looking at a live model comes with a measure of difficulty. However, it can help you increase your skills and adaptability as an artist.

Why would you want to use a live model as a drawing reference?

- As mentioned earlier, you stand to improve as an artist. Depending on how far away your model is from you, you may have to look more intently at them to get a detailed drawing.
- You may have to develop skills in being able to map out a quick sketch, if your model is someone who doesn't know that you're drawing them, and they leave your view or begin to move out of the pose you were drawing.
- You may feel like you're on an adventure, when using a live model, since the result may be greatly affected by your model's behavior and how you adapt to it.

If you want to draw using a live model, know your options. You can ask an acquaintance to pose for you. Be courteous and conscious of their time by coming to a mutual agreement on how long they will sit for you. If possible, try to make sure they are in a pose that they can comfortably keep for the allotted time. They are more likely to squirm and move if they are not comfortable. Try to work quicker than you would if you were drawing from a photo. Start out with a sketch mapping out their form, so that in case something happens and they have to break their pose abruptly, you can try to finish the drawing without them later.

You may spot someone you don't know that you'd like to draw, while you are sitting at the mall or at another crowded public place. If you want to draw them without asking them to pose for you, you will need to work fast; sketching the most important parts first and adding the details later. In these drawings you may have to portray motion, since your subject may be moving while you're drawing them. Remember, that if there's someone you'd like to draw, but you don't think you'll have the time, you can discreetly take a picture (camera phones are so great), and use that as a photo reference.

People are everywhere, so carrying a sketchbook and pencil along with you, wherever you go, may help you create some awesome drawings.

Drawing using a live model review

In Lesson 2 you learned that:

- Drawing a live model may require you to work faster.

- If you ask someone to pose for you, you should agree on how long they will sit for you.
- If you are drawing someone in a crowded place who doesn't know that you are drawing them, it is important to make a quick sketch of their form.
- When using a model, work in the main parts first and the details last.
- If you think that you won't be able to sketch out a drawing of a model quick enough, discreetly snap a picture to use as a reference.

Lesson 3 – Drawing Using Your Imagination

You probably have a great imagination. If you are still a beginner at drawing people, your imagination is probably not the most reliable reference.

You have to train your imagination, in order to get good drawing references from it. What does that mean? What that really means is that you have to practice drawing. Doing exercises, like the ones in the first chapters of this guide, will help you fill your mind with a catalog of good facial features to use, body styles, and how to convey these proportionally.

How will you know when you're ready to let your imagination be your guide? It's sort of like when you were learning to ride a bike.

I started with training wheels. I rode with training wheels for a while, and then when it was evident that I really felt comfortable with that, I got the big kid bike. Of course, I was a bit shaky on that at first; but it wasn't long before I was riding just as well as I did with training wheels. So your photos or live models are your training wheels right now; except you don't have to grow out of using them.

When you're able to create consistently good realistic drawings using your references, you'll know that you can try drawing, using just what you have in your brain. Even if it doesn't look perfect at first, keep trying and you'll get the hang of it.

Your mind is capable of storing an enormous amount of information. Keep practicing drawing people and soon your mind will be one of your greatest resources for drawing inspiration.

Drawing using your imagination

In Lesson 3 you learned that:

- You should practice drawing people from references first, before you draw just using your imagination.
- The more you practice drawing people, the better your memory of realistic proportions will be.
- Use exercises like the ones from earlier in the guide to "train your imagination."

- You will be able to tell that you are ready to try drawing, without references, when you consistently create good work using references.
- When you first start drawing straight from your imagination, it may not be perfect, so keep trying.

Chapter 9: Putting Your New Skills to Use

As you notice improvement in your drawing skills, you may wonder what you can do with what you've learned. There are actually plenty of ways that you can showcase your new talent.

- Take photos of your artwork and share it with friends on your social network profile or through e-mail. It's great to get support and commendation for your hard work from the people who matter most to you. Let them know what you're doing; otherwise they'll have no idea.

- Join a website where other artists can give you feedback and constructive criticism on your artwork. This will help you learn even more and you may be able to help others. You will also get your work out there and it can give you great exposure, if you're looking to sell your artwork.

- If you are looking to profit from your talent, you can set up an online shop on a site like Etsy.com and sell your artwork to people anywhere in the world. Selling online does require that you learn some e-commerce, but there is a lot of free information out there on how to sell your work online.

- If there is a community of artists where you live, try to collaborate and network with them. It is great to have a support group that you can meet with in person. They can share with you tips and help you to see opportunities to contribute to the creative culture where you live.

- Give custom drawings as gifts to friends or relatives. They will treasure your drawings and spread the word about your work.

Those are just a few suggestions that I recommend, to which you should give some thought. Do not feel like you have to join every artsy website and don't overload your friends with constant posts about your artwork. Stay balanced. You should enjoy creating your artwork and sharing it with others; but still do the important things in life, even if drawing people becomes your day job.

Social networking sites make it easy for you to share photos of your artwork with people on your network.

Conclusion

I want to thank you for reading this guide. I was very honored, to be asked to write it. In all honesty, it was a challenge to write and required research and practice on my part. I think that it has helped me to improve my understanding of proportions and the human form.

I sincerely hope that it has been a help to you. Keep practicing the exercises from this guide; I know I will. Remember the old adage, practice makes perfect.

About the Expert

Elise White has been drawing people since she was a tot. Since then, with practice, as well as with guidance from instructors, Elise has been able to make realistic drawings of people. She sells her work and creates custom commissioned pieces online in her Etsy shop, Pieces of Elise's.

Elise also enjoys creating artwork with other mediums such as polymer clay, stoneware, and acrylic paint. She also styles naturally curly hair from her home in Omaha, Nebraska. In all of her endeavors, Elise has learned that in order to get your desired results, when you are trying something new, it is important to keep practicing. If you really love what you're doing, you won't quit when it seems difficult. You'll see it through and all your hard work will pay off.

HowExpert publishes quick 'how to' guides on all topics from A to Z by everyday experts. Visit HowExpert.com to learn more.

Recommended Resources

- HowExpert.com – Quick 'How To' Guides on All Topics from A to Z by Everyday Experts.
- HowExpert.com/free – Free HowExpert Email Newsletter.
- HowExpert.com/books – HowExpert Books
- HowExpert.com/courses – HowExpert Courses
- HowExpert.com/clothing – HowExpert Clothing
- HowExpert.com/membership – HowExpert Membership Site
- HowExpert.com/affiliates – HowExpert Affiliate Program
- HowExpert.com/writers – Write About Your #1 Passion/Knowledge/Expertise & Become a HowExpert Author.
- HowExpert.com/resources – Additional HowExpert Recommended Resources
- YouTube.com/HowExpert – Subscribe to HowExpert YouTube.
- Instagram.com/HowExpert – Follow HowExpert on Instagram.
- Facebook.com/HowExpert – Follow HowExpert on Facebook.